Opposites

Los contrarios

lohs kohn-*trah*-ree-ohs

Illustrated by Clare Beaton

Ilustraciones de Clare Beaton

BARRON'S

big

grande

grahn-deh

little

pequeño, pequeña

peh-*kehn*-yoh, peh-*kehn*-yah

fat

gordo, gorda

gohr-doh, *gohr*-dah

thin

delgado, delgada

dehl-*gah*-doh, dehl-*gah*-dah

hot

caliente

kahl-*yehn*-teh

cold

frío, fría

free-oh, *free*-ah

clean

limpio, limpia

leem-pee-oh, leem-pee-ah

dirty

sucio, sucia

soo-see-oh, *soo*-see-ah

push

empujar

ehm-poo-hahr

pull

tirar

tee-rahr

noisy

ruidoso, ruidosa

roo-ee-*doh*-soh, roo-ee-*doh*-sah

quiet

tranquilo, tranquila

trahn-*kee*-loh, trahn-*kee*-lah

heavy

pesado, pesada

peh-*sah*-doh, peh-*sah*-dah

light

ligero, ligera

lee-*heh*-roh, lee-*heh*-rah

wet

mojado, mojada

moh-*hah*-doh, moh-*hah*-dah

dry

seco, seca

seh-koh, *seh*-kah

happy

contento, contenta

kohn-*tehn*-toh, kohn-*tehn*-tah

sad

triste

trees-teh

empty

vacío, vacía

vah-*see*-oh, vah-*see*-ah

full

lleno, llena

yeh-noh, *yeh*-nah

long

largo, larga

lahr-goh, *lahr*-gah

short

corto, corta

kohr-toh, kohr-tah

A simple guide to pronouncing Spanish words

• Read this guide as naturally as possible, as if it were English.
• Put stress on the letters in *italics*, for example, *kehn* in peh-*kehn*-yoh.

Los contrarios	lohs kohn-*trah*-ree-ohs	**Opposites**
grande	*grahn*-deh	**big**
pequeño, pequeña	peh-*kehn*-yoh, peh-*kehn*-yah	**little**
gordo, gorda	*gohr*-doh, *gohr*-dah	**fat**
delgado, delgada	dehl-*gah*-doh, dehl-*gah*-dah	**thin**
caliente	kahl-*yehn*-teh	**hot**
frío, fría	*free*-oh, *free*-ah	**cold**
limpio, limpia	*leem*-pee-oh, *leem*-pee-ah	**clean**
sucio, sucia	*soo*-see-oh, *soo*-see-ah	**dirty**
empujar	ehm-poo-*hahr*	**push**
tirar	tee-*rahr*	**pull**
ruidoso, ruidosa	roo-ee-*doh*-soh, roo-ee-*doh*-sah	**noisy**
tranquilo, tranquila	trahn-*kee*-loh, trahn-*kee*-lah	**quiet**
pesado, pesada	peh-*sah*-doh, peh-*sah*-dah	**heavy**
ligero, ligera	lee-*heh*-roh, lee-*heh*-rah	**light**
mojado, mojada	moh-*hah*-doh, moh-*hah*-dah	**wet**
seco, seca	*seh*-koh, *seh*-kah	**dry**
contento, contenta	kohn-*tehn*-toh, kohn-*tehn*-tah	**happy**
triste	*trees*-teh	**sad**
vacío, vacía	vah-*see*-oh, vah-*see*-ah	**empty**
lleno, llena	*yeh*-noh, *yeh*-nah	**full**
largo, larga	*lahr*-goh, *lahr*-gah	**long**
corto, corta	*kohr*-toh, *kohr*-tah	**short**